Text Copyright © 2016 by JessicaTilley

Illustration Copyright © 2016 by Saima Riaz

All rights reserved, including the right of reproduction in whole or in part in any form.

For my children and for all children.

Black, Bright, Brown, Light

Do you think I'm beautiful?
Many don't think it's true.

Do you hear them saying things about me?
Will you tell them I'm black, like you?

What's so different about us, by the way, except the color of our skin?

Don't we both sleep and play and eat and read and sing and think and grin?

Will you tell them that long ago the earth was formed and people were put on its face?

It's incredibly foolish and small-minded even, to focus on hair, skin, and creed.

Those genetic factors mean nothing when another is in need.

Remember we all need love from each other as we grow and thrive and reach.

Will you help me please, with this important work? I've got so much to teach.

Should we stick with the initial feelings that exist to keep us from approaching new friends?

Our thoughts should reach far beyond what we see like external features and hair ends.

Let's stop and question our bias. Does our hue make us a particular thing?

The roon is a mindset, a myth, just a lie.
Yet many continue to cling.

We owe it to our future, our present, and our past to be the change we have yet to see.

Set your mind in the right direction.
Which path will you choose?
There is one that leads to what is right.

We will end what's truly ugly when we eliminate our focus on
black, bright, brown, light.

About the Author

Jessica Tilley is an American children's book author. Her other published books are, "You Have To Be Smart If You're Going To Be Tall," "A Mother's Heart," and "Say It!" In addition to working in education with children and youth she also enjoys spending time with her family as well as creating and selling hand-made jewelry. She hopes her books will influence children and their families to grow together by finding different ways to communicate about everyday issues.

www.ingramcontent.com/pod-product-compliance
Lightning Source LLC
Chambersburg PA
CBHW040023050426
42452CB00002B/113